MARTIAL ARTS IN ACTION

KENDO

MARTIAL ARTS IN ACTION

KENDO

BY CAROL ELLIS

Marshall Cavendish
Benchmark
New York

Other Marshall Cavendish Offices:
Marshall Cavendish International (Asia) Private Limited, 1 New Industrial Road, Singapore
536196 • Marshall Cavendish International (Thailand) Co Ltd. 253 Asoke, 12th Flr, Sukhumvit
21 Road, Klongtoey Nua, Wattana, Bangkok 10110, Thailand • Marshall Cavendish (Malaysia)
Sdn Bhd, Times Subang, Lot 46, Subang Hi-Tech Industrial Park, Batu Tiga, 40000 Shah Alam,
Selangor Darul Ehsan, Malaysia

Marshall Cavendish is a trademark of Times Publishing Limited

All websites were available and accurate when this book was sent to press.

Library of Congress Cataloging-in-Publication Data
Ellis, Carol, 1945-
Kendo / Carol Ellis.
p. cm. — (Martial arts in action)
Includes index.
ISBN 978-0-7614-4935-5
1. Kendo—Juvenile literature. I. Title.
GV1142.E55 2011
796.86—dc22
2010013827

Editor: Peter Mavrikis
Publisher: Michelle Bisson
Art Director: Anahid Hamparian
Series design by Kristen Branch
Illustrations by Janet Hamlin

Photo research by Candlepants Incorporated
Cover Photo: Tohoku Color Agency / Getty Images

The photographs in this book are used by permission and through the courtesy of:
Alamy Images: Aflo Foto Agency, 2, 24, 26, 31, 36; Photo Japan, 9, 18; Mary Evans Picture Library, 11; Japan
Art Collection (JAC), 17; Image Source, 19, 22; Inmagine, 20; Pete Jenkins, 28; Nordicphotos, 32;
Kirk Treakle, 33, 38, 41; Richard Levine, 34; Amana Images Inc., 39; Rollie Rodriguez, 42. *Getty Images*:
Shinya Sasaki/Neovision, 6; DEA / A. Dagli Orti, 8, 10, 12; SSPL, 15; Andy Crawford, 30. *Janet Hamlin*: 27.

Printed in Malaysia (T)
1 3 5 6 4 2

CONTENTS

CHAPTER ONE

AN ANCIENT ART

MORE THAN FOUR HUNDRED YEARS AGO, a **samurai** from Japan named Arima Kihei posted a public challenge to a duel: Anyone who thought they could defeat him in a sword fight should sign the challenge and show up at a certain time and place. Duels between samurai were not unusual at the time. The samurai skill with razor-sharp, long-bladed swords made them feared and respected both on and off the battlefield. When they were not fighting wars, they worked on their swordsmanship by practicing **kenjutsu**, the art of the sword. Different masters of sword fighting developed their own schools and styles of fighting. Students who learned from them would often fight duels to test themselves and the different styles.

A YOUNG MARTIAL ARTIST MEDITATES, SURROUNDED BY HER KENDO EQUIPMENT.

One person took on the samurai's challenge. His name was Miyamoto Musashi. Later he wrote, "I have trained in the way of **strategy** since my youth, and at the age of thirteen I fought a duel for the first time. My opponent was called Arima Kihei, and I defeated him." Thirteen-year-old Musashi did not just defeat the samurai, he killed him.

SWORDSMANSHIP WAS AN ESSENTIAL SKILL FOR JAPANESE WARRIORS FOR HUNDREDS OF YEARS.

A MARTIAL ARTIST RAISES HIS SAMURAI SWORD DURING A KENJUTSU DEMONSTRATION.

From that first duel when he was a boy, Musashi went on to become one of the greatest swordsmen in Japanese history. Like many samurai, he traveled the country, fighting duels to **hone** his sword-fighting skills. According to old accounts, he fought at least sixty duels and never lost. He became a legend in his lifetime. He is still a legend. Characters based on Musashi have appeared in movies, books, television series, and video games.

Musashi tried to perfect his strategy and skills because he believed that "strategy is the craft of the warrior." But like many other samurai, he also thought that learning the art of the sword was the key to learning other things in life, such as how to be calm, peaceful, and confident. This idea has lived on as much as Musashi's famous duels. It can be found today in the modern martial art of kendo.

THE HISTORY OF KENDO AND OTHER SWORD ARTS

CHAPTER TWO

KENDO IS THE JAPANESE STYLE of two-handed fencing. It grew out of kenjutsu, the art of the sword. Kenjutsu began more than one thousand years ago. It was practiced by the samurai, or warrior class. Samurai fought battles for rival ruling families and defended the country from invaders. They used many weapons, including bows and arrows and spears. But they became most famous for their skill with the long, curve-bladed **katana** sword.

For hundreds of years, the samurai were the most respected group of people in Japan. At times, only samurai were allowed to have swords. A peasant caught with one would often face death from the very sword he had carried.

A NINETEENTH-CENTURY PHOTOGRAPH SHOWING THREE SAMURAI IN FULL ARMOR.

IN THIS OLD PRINT, TWO SWORDSMEN PRACTICE KENJUTSU AS SPECTATORS LOOK ON.

Knowing how to use a sword well could mean the difference between life and death, and samurai were always trying to perfect their skills and **technique**. During the 1400s, when civil war raged across Japan, different master swordsmen developed their own styles and schools of kenjutsu. By the early 1500s, more than two hundred schools existed. Even during the peaceful time following the civil wars, samurai kept up their training in the art of the sword.

At first, real swords were used in training. But there were so many injuries and deaths that students and teachers began to use gear such as chest and head protectors and heavy gloves. Next came the bamboo sword called the **shinai**, which made training even safer.

Over time, the goal of kenjutsu began to change. Instead of a way to train for battle and defeat an opponent, kenjutsu eventually became

KENDO AND OTHER MARTIAL ARTS HAVE BEEN
TAUGHT IN JAPANESE SCHOOLS FOR MANY YEARS.

a style of martial art that improved a fighter's character as well as his swordsmanship. In the early twentieth century, master swordsmen from different schools came together to develop a new system of kenjutsu. They called it kendo, the way of the sword. By studying kendo, students learn to practice a way of life that strengthens the body, the mind, and the spirit.

NAGINATA

Naginata is another type of Japanese martial art. It gets its name from the weapon that was used during the time of the samurai. A naginata was a wooden pole-like weapon between 5 and 9 feet (1.5–3 meters)

Kenjutsu, Kendo, and Zen Buddhism

Part of samurai kenjutsu training was the study of morals and the religion of Buddhism, especially **Zen Buddhism**. The spiritual side of their training helped them to concentrate and focus so they could be completely aware of every moment. This helped them not only in their personal lives, but in their lives as sword fighters. Even though Zen is not taught as part of kendo today, the concentration, focus, and awareness are important in learning and practicing the art.

long. At one end was a curved blade that was usually about 1 or 2 feet (.3–.6 m) long. The other end had a sharp cap that could pierce between the plates of an enemy's armor. A warrior would swing it in wide, sweeping arcs that kept all but the best fighters from getting past that slashing blade without being wounded or killed. Foot soldiers in the front lines of battle almost always used the naginata. They would injure and disable a horse with it, then use it to kill the rider when the horse fell.

Women also became experts with the naginata, especially women of the warrior class. Samurai women often had to protect their towns

THIS NINETEENTH-CENTURY ENGRAVING BY A EUROPEAN VISITOR SHOWS JAPANESE SOLDIERS TRAINING WITH WOODEN STAFFS.

and homes while men were away fighting battles. Because the naginata was so long, a woman could keep most attackers at a safe distance. During the years of the civil wars, there are stories of women dressed in armor, fighting with the naginata. One story tells of the wife of a warlord who led eighty-three soldiers against the enemy attacking her castle, "whirling her naginata like a waterwheel."

During the years between 1600 and 1800, Japanese women were required to master the naginata by the time they were eighteen. Today, women, men, and young people practice the martial art of naginata in many countries around the world. The study of naginata includes **kata**, a noncombat series of movements that show technical skill. It also has a combat form where athletes score points by hitting an opponent on parts of the body, including the wrist, throat, and stomach. In this form, the athletes wear protective gear, and bamboo has replaced the steel blade. Like most martial arts, naginata builds not only physical strength and **stamina**, but character that comes with concentration and discipline.

IAIDO

Iaido is the art of drawing the sword. It was developed by the samurai during their training in kenjutsu. While kenjutsu and kendo begin with the sword already in hand, iaido begins with the sword still in its sheath. Its goal was to teach someone how to draw the sword and kill an opponent in one smooth move, then return the sword to its sheath.

Today, men, women, and older kids practice iaido to learn sword techniques. It is taught in kata, or forms, as well as with partners, using

THE LEGENDARY FEMALE WARRIOR HANGAKU GOZEN ON HORSEBACK.

THE HISTORY OF KENDO AND OTHER SWORD ARTS ● 17

MARTIAL ARTISTS STAND READY TO DRAW THEIR SWORDS.

wooden swords. Iaido teaches not only skill with the sword, but physical discipline, concentration, and calmness of mind.

ESCRIMA

Escrima is a martial art of the Philippines. It was a combination of stick-fighting and empty-handed combat that was practiced as a type of recreation for generations. But when the Spanish invaded the islands in the sixteenth century, the Filipinos turned it into a powerful fighting art. During their rule of the islands, the Spanish outlawed the practice of escrima. Instead of dying out, escrima went underground.

It was disguised as a part of ritual dances that were often performed to entertain the Spanish! When Spanish rule ended, the ban on escrima was lifted, but it still remained secretive. After World War II, many Filipinos left the islands for the United States and they brought the art of escrima with them. Today, people of all ages study the art for sport and self-defense.

Escrima has many different styles. Most of them focus on learning how to use the escrima stick, a **rattan** that is about 2 feet (.6 m) long and 1 inch (2.5 cm) thick. Some styles use a single stick while others use a stick in each hand. Many styles also teach kicking and striking. Footwork and balance are very important in escrima.

THE TRADITIONAL FILIPINO MARTIAL ART OF ESCRIMA.

CHINESE MARTIAL ARTS

Wushu, the Chinese term for martial arts, began thousands of years ago in ancient China as a way to train soldiers for battle and as a means of self-defense. Over the years, hundreds of styles of martial arts developed, including tai chi chuan and the many different forms of kung fu. Most styles used both hand-to-hand combat and weapons. Today, children and adults around the world study them for exercise, self-defense, and as a sport. Wushu is also presented in noncombat performances. Many of the styles are practiced and performed using four of the traditional Chinese weapons:

SWORDFIGHTING IS AN IMPORTANT PART OF WUSHU, THE CHINESE MARTIAL ARTS.

The staff is called the "father of all weapons" because all other weapons were developed from it.

The saber is called the "marshal of all weapons." It is one of the most used weapons in kung fu.

The spear is known as the "king of all weapons." It was a major military weapon in ancient times.

The straight sword, or the "gentleman of all weapons," is used in most major competitions.

FENCING

Fencing with swords began as a way to train soldiers for battle, but it quickly became a popular sport that goes back thousands of years. An ancient Egyptian carving from about 1200 BCE shows a fencing **bout** in front of judges. The carving shows contestants wearing masks for protection and using weapons fitted with protective tips. Ancient Greek and Roman civilizations all had some form of fencing.

Practicing swordsmanship to prepare for war continued through the years, and so did fencing as a sport. Like the masters of kenjutsu in Japan, fencing masters in Spain, Germany, and Italy organized schools and taught different techniques and moves. By the fifteenth century, fencing had become a popular pastime for European noblemen. But it also became a popular—and deadly—way to settle arguments or avenge insults by dueling. Dueling never completely faded away until after World War I. But by then, most people did not learn to fence so they could duel or fight in wars. They learned it as a fun, competitive sport, and they dueled for points. Fencing is a fast-moving sport and it is often hard for judges to decide if a point has been scored. In many

EUROPEAN-STYLE FENCING IS PRACTICED AS A COMPETITIVE SPORT ALL OVER THE WORLD.

competitions, fencers wear sensors that register points electronically whenever a sword makes contact. Fencers always wear protective gear on their faces and bodies.

Fencing has been part of the modern Olympic Games since 1896. Wheelchair fencing, for amputees or people with spinal injuries, was introduced to the Paralympic Games in 1960. Today fencing is taught in clubs, most colleges, and many high schools and is practiced by men, women, teens, and children around the world.

The three basic types of fencing are set apart by three different weapons.

The foil is a light, flexible blade that is about 35 inches (89 cm) long. A fencer scores a point by touching the tip of the blade to the opponent's **torso**.

The epee is about as long as the foil. But it is stiffer and twice as heavy. A fencer scores a point by touching the tip of the blade anywhere on an opponent's body.

The saber is about the same size as the foil. A saber fencer can use both the tip and the cutting edge to score points. The target area is anywhere from the opponent's waist up to the top of the head.

CLOTHING AND EQUIPMENT

UNIFORM

A kendo uniform is called a **kendogi**. It consists of a cotton top and long, pleated skirt-like pants. Kendogi are usually dark blue or black. Some beginning students wear white tops. Kendo is practiced in bare feet.

ARMOR

Bogu, or armor, is worn over the kendogi. It is made up of four pieces:

The *men*, or head guard, has a metal face grill and protective flaps that cover the throat, the shoulders, and the back of the head.

A KENDOKA HOLDING HIS BOKKEN.

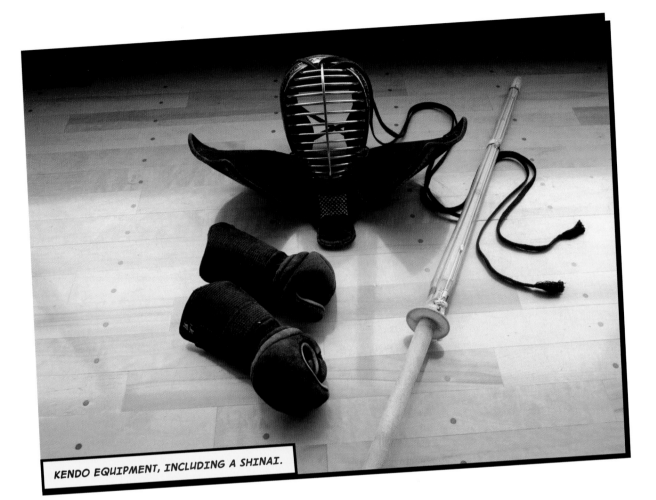

KENDO EQUIPMENT, INCLUDING A SHINAI.

The *do* protects the torso and is made from bamboo covered in leather.

The *kote* are thickly padded gloves or mitts that protect the hands, wrists, and forearms.

The *tare* covers the waist, hips, and groin. It is a thick cotton belt with protective flaps hanging from it.

SWORDS

The *shinai* is made of four slats of dried bamboo, wrapped in leather and held together by a string. It is used in practice and **sparring**.

men

shinai

do

kote

tare

EVERYTHING THE KENDOKA WEARS OR CARRIES HAS A SPECIAL PURPOSE.

The *bokken* is a solid wooden sword made from oak or other hardwood. It is used for kata, or forms.

If you are new to kendo, you will need a shinai to practice with. In many **dojos**, you can start by wearing sweatpants and a T-shirt. Later, you will need a kendo uniform. As your skills and technique improve, you will need bogu for safety.

LEARNING KENDO

Students of kendo are called **kendoka**. New students begin by learning some of the basics such as **etiquette**, posture, footwork, and how to swing the shinai, or bamboo sword.

BAMBOO SHINAI SWORDS WAITING TO BE USED.

Etiquette is an important part of kendo class. Students bow at the beginning and end of class, to their **sensei** and to their training partners. The bow, or *rei*, shows respect for the dojo, the teacher, and each other.

An upright posture keeps you ready for offensive and defensive movements. Your feet should be underneath your hips and your hips underneath your shoulders. Your feet should be parallel, with your left foot slightly behind the right. If you are off-balance, you will not be able to deliver a good strike, and it will be easier for an opponent to strike you.

Footwork is one of the most important parts of good kendo technique. Students learn to slide their feet as they move and to keep their heels slightly raised so they are always ready to attack or retreat. Movement can be made forwards, backwards, to the left, to the right, and on the diagonal.

The shinai is held in a two-handed grip. The proper grip gives you strength when you strike and keeps you from dropping your sword or having it knocked from your hands.

Suburi are swinging and striking techniques. They are practiced without armor. Students swing the shinai through the air while moving forwards and backwards, then strike at an imaginary target. Suburi develop stamina and technique, and are practiced over and over by all students.

Kiai is an explosive shout. In practice and competition, kendoka shout the name of their target whenever they make a strike. The kiai is a way of building up and focusing all your spirit and energy into a single movement.

THIS YOUNG KENDOKA IS HOLDING AN IAIDO SWORD.

Kata, or forms, are prearranged movements that help students practice the moves they have learned. Kata are performed with a partner, with wooden swords and without armor.

When students are ready to begin training with armor, they improve their skills by learning more techniques. These may include the following.

Kiri-kaeshi: Working with a partner, students learn to strike the *men*, or head, in the center, on the top left and the top right.

Uchi-komi: Partners practice their skills on each other. Each one alternates between being the attacker and the defender.

Kakari-geiko: This exercise lets students practice all their skills

MANY YEARS OF RELENTLESS PRACTICE ARE NECESSARY TO PERFECT KENDO SKILLS.

against a partner without worrying about being attacked. It is a one-sided fight that builds stamina and strength.

Ji-geiko: Free-sparring lets students put all their skills to the test against a partner. This time, the partner will fight back.

Kendo uses a ranking system to show a student's level of achievement. Kendoka are split into two groups, kyu and **dan**, or student and master. Students begin at the sixth kyu and rise to the first. There are ten dan levels. Students start at the first dan and rise to the tenth. To rise to a new level, students need to show that they have learned certain skills and techniques. Most kendo dojos do not give

colored belts to show rankings. Everyone wears the same clothes in the same colors. If you want to know someone's rank, the best way is to watch them fight!

STRIKE ZONES

There are three main target areas in kendo:

The *kote* or forearm.

Either side of the *do,* or torso.

The top or either side of the *men,* or head.

KENDO STUDENTS MAY BE YOUNG OR OLD.

TOURNAMENT COMPETITION HELPS KENDOKA TO STRENGTHEN AND TEST THEIR SKILLS.

The throat is a fourth target area, but a thrust to the throat can be very dangerous, and only older, advanced students are allowed to practice it.

Strikes on any other part of the body are not legal and do not score points in competition.

TOURNAMENTS

Competition in tournaments is a way for kendoka to test themselves and their techniques against others. Competition is called **shiai** and is held in front of referees who judge whether a strike is successful. For a strike to be successful, three things must happen at the same time: the shinai must hit the target soundly, the attacker's front foot must hit the floor with a loud stamp, and the kendoka must give out a spirited *kiai!*

A kendo *shiai* lasts for five minutes. A strike is worth one point. The first contestant to score two points wins the match.

Kendo tournaments are held at the international, national, and local levels. There are fourteen kendo regions in the United States, and each region develops its own team for the national championship. Many clubs hold tournaments with other clubs or between members of their own club.

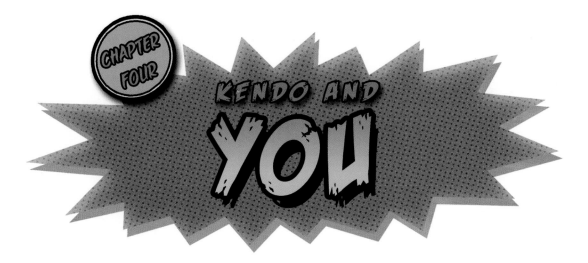

CHAPTER FOUR

KENDO AND YOU

IF YOU WANT TO LEARN KENDO, the first thing to do is find a dojo, or training hall. Many martial arts dojos and clubs offer kendo, and many colleges and universities have classes that are open to the public. The yellow pages or a computer search can help you find clubs in your area. The All United States Kendo Federation, the governing body of kendo in the United States, also has a listing of kendo clubs. Many of the clubs have websites that tell you what the classes will be like and what kind of equipment you will need. If you can, try to visit a dojo to watch a class and talk to the sensei, or teacher, to get an idea of what to expect.

Kendo has always been popular in Japan, where most high schools

THE ART OF KENDO HAS SPREAD FAR BEYOND ITS ORIGINS IN JAPAN.

A YOUNG JAPANESE KENDOKA.

and many middle schools have kendo clubs. But its popularity has grown way beyond Japan. Today, forty-seven countries belong to the International Kendo Federation and millions of people around the world practice the way of the sword.

Almost anyone can learn kendo. You do not have to be strong, muscular, or tall. Size does not matter and neither does age. Kids as young as eight and adults in their sixties have joined kendo classes. Some do it for fun or as a sport. Others try to become masters of the art. No matter why they study kendo, most people find that they get

THE STUDY OF KENDO MAY BEGIN IN CHILDHOOD AND LAST A LIFETIME.

THE FOUR POISONS OF KENDO

Fear, doubt, surprise, and confusion are called the four "poisons" of kendo.

Fear can make a person stop thinking.

Doubt can make a person lose confidence.

Surprise can make a person lose focus.

Confusion can make a person hesitate.

People who study kendo learn to battle these "poisons" not just in sword fighting, but often in daily life.

KENDO DEMANDS MENTAL DISCIPLINE, AS WELL AS PHYSICAL SKILL.

much more out of it than learning how to swing a bamboo sword.

Kendo gives your muscles and your **cardiovascular** system a great workout. In kendo, you learn to shut out distractions and focus your mind only on what you are doing. If you can do it in kendo, you can do it in other things like schoolwork.

Practicing kendo is a challenge, but it builds confidence and self-esteem. Working on a single move over and over again can be tiring. But when you keep at it and succeed, you feel full of energy and ready for the next challenge!

MANY PEOPLE, LIKE THESE BOYS IN JAPAN, FORM LIFELONG FRIENDSHIPS BY PRACTICING KENDO WITH ONE ANOTHER.

People who train together in kendo often develop strong friend-ships. As a high school-age student of kendo said, "You will learn that the kids in your kendo club will become some of your best friends, and they will always be there if you need help—in kendo and in daily life." Learning to respect yourself and other people can help you deal with many social situations throughout your life.

GLOSSARY

bogu—The armor worn in kendo.

bokken—A wooden sword.

bout—A contest between two people.

cardiovascular—Involving the heart and blood vessels.

dan—A level of ability, or grade, in many martial arts.

dojo—A martial arts training hall.

etiquette—A code of behavior.

hone—To make more intense or effective.

kata—Forms or movements.

katana—A single-edged, curved sword.

kendogi—The uniform worn in kendo.

kendoka—A person who practices kendo.

kenjutsu—The art of the sword.

kiai—A shout used in kendo when making a strike.

rattan—A hard, durable, and lightweight stem that is similar to bamboo and comes from a vine-like plant.

samurai—A Japanese warrior.

sensei—Teacher.

shiai—Competition.

shinai—The bamboo sword used in kendo.

sparring—Fighting against an opponent.

stamina—Physical strength and endurance.

strategy—A plan of action for accomplishing a goal.

suburi—Swinging and striking techniques.

technique—A method or specific way of doing something.

torso—The upper part of the human body, not including the head and arms.

Zen Buddhism—A religion with believers who focus on meditation and prefer to live a simple life of peace.

FIND OUT MORE

BOOKS

O'Shei, Tim. *Kendo*. Mankato, Minnesota: Capstone Press, 2008.

Scandiffio, Laura. *The Martial Arts Book*. Toronto: Annick Press, 2003.

Slade, Suzanne. *Fencing for Fun*. Mankato, Minnesota: Compass Point Books, 2008.

WEBSITES

The All United States Kendo Federation
http://www.auskf.info/

Kendo America
http://www.kendo-usa.org

Kids Web Japan
http://web-japan.org/kidsweb/meet/kendo/index.html\

United States Naginata Federation
http://www.naginata.org/usnf/usnf.html

USA Fencing
http://www.usfencing.org/

INDEX

ABOUT THE AUTHOR

In addition to kendo, Carol Ellis has written about the martial arts of judo and jujitsu and wrestling, as well as books about pets and endangered animals. Her favorite sport is baseball. She lives in the Hudson Valley in New York.